21st Century Junior Library

Tape Measures

By Katie Marsico

CHERRY LAKE PUBLISHING * ANN ARBOR, MICHIGAN

Published in the United States of America by Cherry Lake Publishing
Ann Arbor, Michigan
www.cherrylakepublishing.com

Content Adviser: Roger McGregor, Director, Hannibal Career & Technical Center, Hannibal, Missouri

Reading Adviser: Marla Conn, ReadAbility, Inc.

Photo Credits: Cover, ©auremar/Shutterstock, Inc.; page 4, ©iStockphoto.com/diego_cervo; page 6, ©Laborant/Shutterstock, Inc.; page 8, ©Robert Crum/Shutterstock, Inc.; page 10, ©arek_malang/Shutterstock, Inc.; page 12, ©isak55/Shutterstock, Inc.; page 14, ©Nancy Hixson/Shutterstock, Inc.; page 16, ©iStockphoto.com/Leontura; page 18, ©iStockphoto.com/alejandrophotography; page 20, ©Dennis MacDonald/Alamy.

LIBRARY OF CONGRESS CATALOGING-IN-PUBLICATION DATA
Marsico, Katie, 1980–
  Tape measures/by Katie Marsico.
      pages cm.—(Basic tools) (21st century junior library)
  Audience: K to grade 3.
  Includes bibliographical references and index.
  ISBN 978-1-62431-173-4 (library binding)—ISBN 978-1-62431-305-9 (paperback)—
ISBN 978-1-62431-239-7 (e-book)
  1. Tape measures—Juvenile literature. I. Title.
  TJ1313.M365 2013
  681'.2—dc23   2013008333

Cherry Lake Publishing would like to acknowledge the work of
The Partnership for 21st Century Skills.
Please visit www.p21.org *for more information.*

Printed in the United States of America
Corporate Graphics Inc.
July 2013
CLFA13

CONTENTS

People often use tape measures before painting
or building.

What Is a Tape Measure?

Have your parents measured a room before painting it? Has your doctor or gym teacher ever measured your waist? Chances are that they did not use a straight ruler. Instead, they probably used a tape measure.

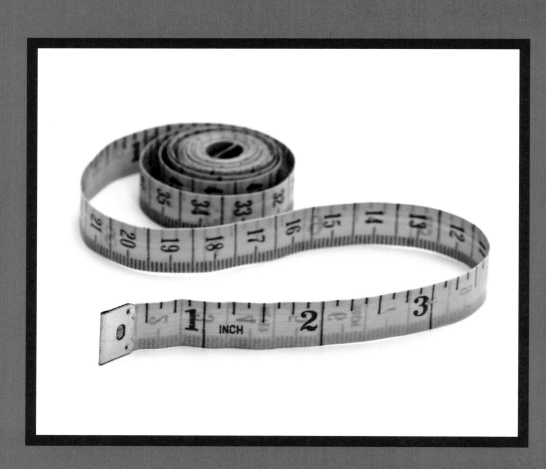

Some tape measures show inches on one side
and centimeters on the other.

A tape measure is a **flexible** ruler. It is marked with lines. The lines show **units** of measurement. The units might be inches or centimeters. They can also include feet or meters. The tape measure can be made from different materials. It is usually paper, plastic, cloth, or metal.

Make a Guess!

Try measuring around your waist with a straight ruler. Is it difficult? Try to guess why. Look at your waist. Is it curved? Can the straight ruler curve with your waist?

Tape measures are handy when measuring around something, such as a tree.

Tape measures can wrap around an object. This makes it easier to measure objects that are curved. Tape measures are usually longer than straight rulers. Some tape measures even reach the height of skyscrapers!

Tape measures can help mark a certain distance along a wall or other object.

How Are Tape Measures Used?

A person first stretches a tape measure across or around an object. Then the person reads the lines marking units of measurement. These show how long or wide the object is.

A hook at the end of a tape measure curves around the edge of an object. This keeps the tape in place.

Sometimes a metal hook is at one end of the tape. The rest of the tape coils into a small case. The hook holds the tape in place when someone takes measurements. **Retractable** tape measures have **springs** in their cases. The springs pull the tape into the case.

Look!

Do your parents own a tape measure? Ask to see it. What units of measurement are marked? Does it have more than one unit marked?

A person turns the metal hand crank on the side of this tape measure to roll up the tape.

Some tape measures are long but have no springs. They sometimes have a **hand crank** instead. Turning it winds the tape up.

Certain tape measures use lasers to take measurements. Some tape measures have computer screens. The screens show **digital** measurement readings.

A tailor often measures a person's
arms, back, neck, and waist.

Different Kinds of Tape Measures

People use different tape measures for different jobs. Sewing tape measures are usually marked in inches and centimeters. They are made from cloth, paper, or plastic. Tailors use them to measure a person's body. Then they can make clothes that are a perfect fit!

Retractable tape measures are sometimes used when constructing buildings.

People use retractable tape measures for home projects. These tape measures help measure floors, walls, and ceilings. They are often longer than sewing tape measures. They also have a button. Pressing it locks the tape in place. This helps if a person needs to let go of the tape measure.

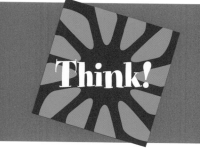

Think!

Tape measures help people get exact measurements. Why do you think this is important? What if a person just guessed how to make clothes to fit you. What would your clothes look like?

The long jump event in track and field requires careful measurements of how far a person jumped.

Reel tape measures are made from thin steel, or plastic. They often have a hand crank. People use them to measure very long distances. Measuring sports fields is one example. Can you imagine measuring a football field with a straight ruler? These flexible tools make measuring much easier!

GLOSSARY

digital (DI-juh-tuhl) involving computer technology

flexible (FLEK-suh-buhl) able to bend

hand crank (HAND KRAYNGK) a handle that is attached to a shaft and turned by hand

retractable (ri-TRAK-tuh-buhl) able to be pulled inward or folded into a storable size or shape

springs (SPRINGZ) spiral coils of metal that return to their original shape after being stretched or pressed down

units (YOO-nits) amounts used as a standard of measurement

FIND OUT MORE

BOOK

Metz, Lorijo. *Using Rulers and Tape Measures*. New York: PowerKids Press, 2013.

WEB SITES

eHow: Types of Tape Measures

www.ehow.com/list_5925448 _types-tape-measures.html
Get a closer look at the different kinds of tape measures.

Fit Just Right: Printable Tape Measures

www.fitjustright.com/Download /tapeMeasures.pdf
Print out the pieces of a paper tape measure and glue them together to start taking some measurements of your own!

How Stuff Works: Tape Measure

http://home.howstuffworks.com/tape -measure.htm
Find out more about what a tape measure does and how to take care of this tool.

INDEX

ABOUT THE AUTHOR

Katie Marsico is the author of more than 100 children's books. She lives in a suburb of Chicago, Illinois, with her husband and children.